OUTSMART MATH

for ages 10 & up

MARK SHULMAN

KAPLAN

PUBLISHING

New York

Vice President and Publisher: Maureen McMahon
Editorial Director: Jennifer Farthing
Development Editor: Kate Lopaze
Production Editor: Fred Urfer
Illustrations: Aaron Meshon
Photography: Veer, Inc
Typesetting: Pamela Beaulieu
Interior design: Carly Schnur

Published by Kaplan Publishing, a division of Kaplan, Inc.
1 Liberty Plaza, 24th Floor
New York, NY 10006

May 2008
10 9 8 7 6 5 4 3 2 1

ISBN-13: 978-1-4195-5201-4

Kaplan Publishing books are available at special quantity discounts to use for sales promotions, employee premiums, or educational purposes. Please email our Special Sales Department to order or for more information at kaplanpublishing@kaplan.com, or write to Kaplan Publishing, 1 Liberty Plaza, 24th Floor, New York, NY 10006.

WHAT'S OUTSMART MATH ALL ABOUT?

Congratulations! You're the proud owner (or reader) of the very finest *Outsmart Math* book you've ever seen. We know you're itching to open it up and take it for a spin...but first, please read this totally complicated introduction. We're sure you have a lot of questions about the book before you read all the questions in the book. Here are some questions we hope you'll ask.

WILL this book answer all of my questions?

That depends on what all your questions are. But it will answer all *our* questions—250 of them, if you're counting. And if our answers happen to match your questions, then the answer is a resounding YES!

HOW, exactly, do I use my new Outsmart book?

First of all, there are two questions on a page. But that's not all. Turn the page, and presto—you'll find two answers. That's twice the value! When you get to the end of a section, there are two bonus questions (we call them "bonus questions") for an extra challenge. When you finally get to the end of each section, take a victory lap around the building. Exercise is good for refreshing brain cells. Then you can move on to the next set of questions.

WHO is Mark Shulman, and WHAT makes him an authority on this topic?

Mark Shulman is the author of dozens (12s) of books for people just like you. His books have titles like *The Brainiac Box: 600 Facts Every Smart Person Should Know* AND *Attack of the Killer Video Book* AND *Mom and Dad Are Palindromes* AND *Secret Hiding Places (for Clever Kids)*. He took math in middle school and can still pass it today!

QUESTION 1

WHAT is infinity?

ANSWER > > > >

• • • • • • • • • •

QUESTION 2

WHAT is a point?

ANSWER > > > >

OUTSMART MATH

Infinity is an amount with no limit or boundaries. The universe is infinite. A line can be infinite. And the last class of the day may seem infinite, but it usually isn't.

• • • • • • • • •

ANSWER 2

A point is the only zero-dimensional object there is, so it's understandably quite small. A point is handy for locating a single place in a plane or in space. And that's the point.

QUESTION 3

WHAT is a line?

ANSWER > > > >

• • • • • • • • •

QUESTION 4

WHAT is a ray (not a stingray—the mathematical term)?

ANSWER > > > >

OUTSMART MATH

ANSWER **3**

A line is two or more points that are infinite—meaning they can continue in either direction for infinity.

• • • • • • • • • •

ANSWER **4**

A ray is a part of a line, with a single endpoint, that can be continued in only one direction for infinity—and beyond.

QUESTION 5

HOW does a line segment compare to a line?

ANSWER > > > >

· · · · · · · · · ·

QUESTION 6

HOW do you define an angle?

ANSWER > > > >

OUTSMART MATH

ANSWER 5

A line segment is the part of a line that exists
between any two points. The points may be close
or the points may be far, but sadly, line segments
do not go on for infinity. They are finite.

• • • • • • • • • •

ANSWER 6

An angle is the figure that's formed when two lines
(or rays) meet (or diverge) at a common endpoint.
The end.

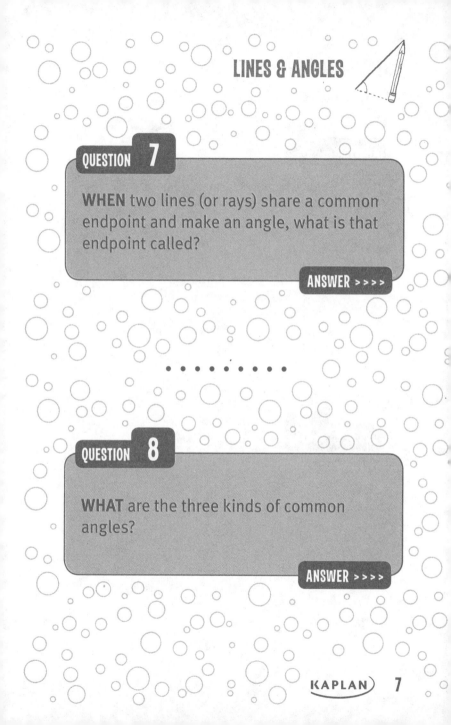

QUESTION 7

WHEN two lines (or rays) share a common endpoint and make an angle, what is that endpoint called?

ANSWER > > > >

QUESTION 8

WHAT are the three kinds of common angles?

ANSWER > > > >

OUTSMART MATH

ANSWER 7

It is a vertex. Vertex is a Latin word meaning whirlpool. (Bet your principal doesn't know that one!)

• • • • • • • • •

ANSWER 8

Common angles are obtuse, acute, or just right. (More on them later.)

QUESTION 9

WHICH unit of measurement is specifically used with angles?

ANSWER >>>>

. . . .

QUESTION 10

WHAT are acute angles, and why are they cute?

ANSWER >>>>

OUTSMART MATH

ANSWER 9

Angles are measured in degrees.

. . . .

ANSWER 10

Acute angles are cute because they're small. Any positive angle that measures between 0 and 90 degrees is called acute.

QUESTION 11

WHAT is an obtuse angle?

ANSWER > > > >

• • • • • • • • •

QUESTION 12

WHERE on your angle is a bisector?

ANSWER > > > >

OUTSMART MATH

An obtuse angle is any positive angle that measures between 91 and 180 degrees.

• • • • • • • • • •

A bisector is a line (or line segment) that bisects (or divides) your angle into two equal parts.
(bi = two and sect = sections.)

QUESTION 13

WHAT is another name for an angle of zero degrees?

ANSWER > > > >

• • • • • • • • • •

QUESTION 14

WHAT is another name for an angle of 180 degrees?

ANSWER > > > >

ANSWER 13

Another name for a zero-degree angle is a ray.

• • • • • • • • •

ANSWER 14

Another name for a 180-degree angle is a line.

QUESTION 15

WHAT is a right angle?

ANSWER > > > >

• • • • • • • • • •

QUESTION 16

WHAT are congruent angles?

ANSWER > > > >

OUTSMART MATH

ANSWER 15

A right angle is an angle that measures precisely 90 degrees; no more, no less. The capital letter L is a right angle.

• • • • • • • • • •

ANSWER 16

Congruent angles are angles that have the same size and shape—but they sometimes smell different.

QUESTION 17

WHAT is a complementary angle?

ANSWER > > > >

. . . .

QUESTION 18

WHAT are supplementary angles?

ANSWER > > > >

OUTSMART MATH

If you combine two angles, and their sum is exactly 90 degrees, you get a complementary angle. Right on.

• • • • • • • • •

Any two angles are supplementary when their sum is precisely 180 degrees—and that's right on the line.

QUESTION 19

WHAT is a straight angle?

ANSWER > > > >

• • • • • • • • •

QUESTION 20

WHAT is an exterior angle?

ANSWER > > > >

OUTSMART MATH

ANSWER 19

Get it straight—it's a straight line. It's 180 degrees.
It's a pair of supplementary angles. It's all of the
above. Apparently, mathematicians never get
bored coming up with new names.

· · · · · · · · ·

ANSWER 20

Let's say you've just measured an angle on
the inside of a triangle. The exterior angle is
located at the same corner, but measured from
the outside. The sum of the interior and exterior
angles will be 180 degrees because they will
always equal a straight line. Interior, exterior...
the more, the merrier.

QUESTION 21

WHAT do adjacent angles share?

ANSWER > > > >

. . . .

QUESTION 22

WHAT do you call an angle with its vertex in the center of a circle?

ANSWER > > > >

OUTSMART MATH

ANSWER 21

Adjacent angles share a side and a vertex. Think about the Leaning Tower of Pisa for a moment. It leans in one direction, making an acute angle. It leans away from the other direction, making an obtuse angle, too. Those acute and obtuse angles are the adjacent angles, and the tower itself is the side they share.

· · · · · · · · ·

ANSWER 22

The word center is the clue. It's a central angle.

QUESTION 23

WHAT do you get when you add up all the interior angles in a triangle?

ANSWER > > > >

• • • • • • • • •

QUESTION 24

HOW many degrees (at the most) are in an acute triangle's angles?

ANSWER > > > >

OUTSMART MATH

ANSWER 23

You get bored, because the three angles will always, always, always total 180 degrees.

• • • • • • • • • •

ANSWER 24

An acute triangle is made up of three acute angles. Each of those angles must measure less than 90 degrees.

QUESTION 25

WHEN is a triangle an isosceles triangle?

ANSWER >>>>

• • • • • • • • • •

QUESTION 26

WHICH triangle actually has three equal sides?

ANSWER >>>>

OUTSMART MATH

ANSWER 25

When a triangle has two sides of the same length, it's an isosceles triangle. The word comes from the Greek *isoskeles*, which means "with equal sides."

• • • • • • • • •

ANSWER 26

Now you're talking about the equilateral triangle. Equilateral means equal sides, too. And it's got three of them.

QUESTION 27

WHAT do you call a triangle that has no equal sides?

ANSWER >>>>

QUESTION 28

WHAT else, besides a right angle, does a triangle need in order to be a right triangle?

ANSWER >>>>

OUTSMART MATH

ANSWER **27**

A triangle with no equal sides is a scalene triangle.

• • • • • • • • • •

ANSWER **28**

Nothing. That's right, nothing. A triangle with a right angle is called a right triangle.

QUESTION 29

WHAT do you call the two sides of a right triangle that aren't the hypotenuse?

ANSWER >>>>

• • • • • • • • •

QUESTION 30

WHAT is up with vertical angles?

ANSWER >>>>

OUTSMART MATH

You call them the legs of the right triangle. Every triangle can be measured in feet, but only the right triangle gets to have legs.

• • • • • • • • • •

Vertical angles are the two nonadjacent angles you get when any two lines meet. The letter X has two pairs of vertical angles.

QUESTION 31

WHAT is the term for the measurement of a straight line's steepness, or incline?

ANSWER > > > >

. . . .

QUESTION 32

WHICH two factors are considered when you calculate a line's slope value?

ANSWER > > > >

OUTSMART MATH

We're inclined to say that a line's steepness is the line's slope. The higher the slope value, the steeper the incline.

• • • • • • • • • •

A slope is the ratio of the line's rise divided by the line's run. It is generally expressed as a ratio, using any two points on the line.

QUESTION 33

WHAT is a line's rise, and what is a line's run?

ANSWER > > > >

. . . .

QUESTION 34

WHAT is a gradient?

ANSWER > > > >

ANSWER 33

The line's rise is the higher point—literally, its vertical rise from the base line. A line's run is its distance across the base line. You're getting into right angle territory here. Imagine a water park slide that's 30 feet high (rise). The slide runs 40 feet along the ground (run). Using the Pythagorean formula $a^2 + b^2 = c^2$ the slide/hypotenuse/slope ends up being 50 feet.

• • • • • • • • • •

ANSWER 34

A gradient is another word for a slope.

QUESTION 35

WHAT do you call two lines, side by side, with the exact same slope?

ANSWER > > > >

• • • • • • • • •

QUESTION 36

WHICH common hand tool is the very definition of the word perpendicular?

ANSWER > > > >

OUTSMART MATH

ANSWER **35**

They're parallel lines. If they ever intersect, or even try to intersect, they're no longer parallel.

• • • • • • • •

ANSWER **36**

Because perpendicular lines come together to form a right angle, you could say the hammer nails the answer nicely.

QUESTION 37

HOW many right angles are in the U.S. flag?

ANSWER > > > >

• • • • • • • • •

QUESTION 38

WHICH part of a playground slide is the hypotenuse: the vertical ladder, the horizontal pavement, or the angled slide?

ANSWER > > > >

OUTSMART MATH

ANSWER 37

There are 56 right angles...that's right. Each stripe has 4 corners × 13 stripes. That's 52, and the box of stars has another 4.

• • • • • • • • •

ANSWER 38

The slide is the right answer. The ladder and the pavement form the right angle. And the line opposite a right triangle's right angle is always the hypotenuse.

QUESTION 39

HOW do you define an equation?

ANSWER > > > >

• • • • • • • •

QUESTION 40

WHAT is something like $Z*(n)^2 + c$ called if it doesn't have an equal sign? (You don't have to solve it to know the answer.)

ANSWER > > > >

ANSWER 39

An equation is a mathematical sentence that includes an equal sign. $2 + 2 = 4$ is an equation. $Z*(n)^2 + c$ is not.

• • • • • • • • • •

ANSWER 40

It's called an expression. Any freestanding calculation or formula is an expression, including lots of words we will cover in this book: exponents, fractions, sums, differences, products, quotients, roots, and more. If the numbers or variables exist on their own, without trying to prove anything, that's an expression.

QUESTION 41

WHAT is a variable?

ANSWER > > > >

. . . .

QUESTION 42

WHAT is a formula?

ANSWER > > > >

OUTSMART MATH

ANSWER **41**

If you like mysteries, you'll like variables. In algebra, they're the unknown and are often represented by a letter, such as the letter x. Variables can be used in expressions (you have x pages of homework) or equations ($x + 2 = 3$).

• • • • • • • • • •

ANSWER **42**

A formula is an equation that states a rule, proves a fact, and helps you plug in certain information to find a specific answer. The formula for determining the length of a hypotenuse, for instance, will always be $a^2 + b^2 = c^2$.

QUESTION 43

WHAT is the name of the formula for determining the length of a hypotenuse?

ANSWER > > > >

• • • • • • • • •

QUESTION 44

WHAT does it mean to square a number?

ANSWER > > > >

ANSWER 43

It's the Pythagorean theorem, created by the ancient Greek mathematician Pythagoras. As you may remember, the formula is $a^2 + b^2 = c^2$. What it means is that you have to square the length of each of the right triangle's two legs (a and b) and add them up, to get the length of the hypotenuse (c).

• • • • • • • • •

ANSWER 44

Squaring a number means multiplying the number by itself. For example, 2 squared is $(2^2) = 2 \times 2 = 4$; 3 squared is $(3^2) = 3 \times 3 = 9$; 5 squared is $(5^2) = 25$; 100 squared is $(100^2) = 10,000$; and $100,000^2 = 10,000,000,000$. (That's 10 billion—a lot of round zeros for a squared number.)

QUESTION 45

WHICH number in 2^3 is the exponent?

ANSWER > > > >

. . . .

QUESTION 46

WHAT is the role of the 2 in 2^3?

ANSWER > > > >

ANSWER 45

The little 3 is the exponent. It represents the number of times that you multiply 2 by itself. In this case, $2^3 = 2 \times 2 \times 2 = 8$.

• • • • • • • • •

ANSWER 46

The 2 is called the base number. This is the number you will be multiplying.

QUESTION 47

HOW would you say the term 2^3 to your teacher?

ANSWER >>>>

. . . .

QUESTION 48

WHAT does "to the power of three" mean?

ANSWER >>>>

OUTSMART MATH

You would say "two cubed." Cubed is the word used when you multiply a number by itself three times.

• • • • • • • • • •

It is yet another way of saying that something is cubed. Incidentally, 10^{33} is 10 to the power of 33.

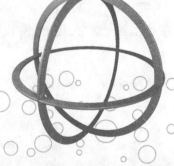

QUESTION 49

WHAT is a table?

ANSWER > > > >

· · · · · · · · · ·

QUESTION 50

WHAT do you call each of the boxes that make up a table?

ANSWER > > > >

OUTSMART MATH

ANSWER 49

Some tables are for serving breakfast, lunch, and dinner on. Mathematical tables serve up data differently than graphs. They're visual aids for organizing and displaying information. Tables organize the information into columns and rows, making a grid. Calendars are the classic table: Each day of the week is a column and each seven-day week is a row.

• • • • • • • • • •

ANSWER 50

They're the basic units of a table, and you call them cells. Each piece of information should stay in its cell—and it doesn't get time off for good behavior.

QUESTION 51

WHAT is a term?

ANSWER > > > >

• • • • • • • • •

QUESTION 52

WHAT is an operator?

ANSWER > > > >

OUTSMART MATH

A term is a part of an expression separated by a plus or minus sign, like $x + 5$, where x is a term and 5 is a term. A term can also be part of a sequence of numbers such as 1, 2, 2, 3, and 92, which has five terms.

• • • • • • • • •

Don't get the wrong number: an operator is a symbol that denotes an operation. $+, -, \times, \div$ are all operators.

QUESTION 53

WHAT is an algebraic expression?

ANSWER > > > >

• • • • • • • • •

QUESTION 54

WHICH of these is a monomial:
$3x^2$, x^2, or 59?

ANSWER > > > >

ANSWER 53

It is a mathematical phrase that can contain numbers and/or variables and at least one operation.

• • • • • • • • •

ANSWER 54

All of them. Monomials are single expressions in algebra that are not connected to any other expressions (or terms) by addition or subtraction. (Mono = one, nomial = term.)

QUESTION **55**

WHAT is a polynomial?

ANSWER >>>>

· · · · · · · · · ·

QUESTION **56**

WHAT is the name for a polynomial with two terms?

ANSWER >>>>

ANSWER 55

A polynomial is an expression containing a monomial or the sum or difference of two or more monomials (or terms). $3x^2 + x^2 - 59$ is a polynomial. So is $a^2b^3 - bc^3$ and even good old 5 + 5. (Poly = many, nomial = term.)

• • • • • • • • •

ANSWER 56

It is a binomial. Binomials have just two terms. Trinomials have just three terms. They're both polynomials. $3x^2 + x^3$ is a binomial. $3x^2 + x^3 - 59$ is a trinomial. (Bi = two, nomial = term, tri = three, nomial = term, etc.)

QUESTION **57**

WHAT are six operations that you may use to solve algebraic problems?

ANSWER > > > >

• • • • • • • • •

QUESTION **58**

WHEN attacking a problem like $3x^2 + x^2 - 59 = 32$, what is the order of operations (or which part of the expression do you simplify first, second, third, etc.)?

ANSWER > > > >

OUTSMART MATH

Alphabetically, the operations are addition, division, exponents, multiplication, roots, and subtraction.

· · · · · · · · ·

Mathematically, the order of operations (the order in which the six operations are evaluated) is to first solve the exponents and roots; then tackle the multiplication and division; and finally, undertake the addition and subtraction portion. Then you take a nice, long rest.

QUESTION 59

WHAT are equivalent equations?

ANSWER > > > >

• • • • • • • • •

QUESTION 60

WHAT is an algorithm?

ANSWER > > > >

ANSWER 59

As you might expect, they're two equations whose solutions are identical—which is identical to the meaning of equivalent. $4^2 + 2^2 = 3^3 - 7$ is an example you can solve in your head.

ANSWER 60

It's an organized procedure for performing a calculation. You could also say it's a specific way to solve a problem. 3^3 is your problem. $3^3 = 3 \times 3 \times 3 = 27$ is your algorithm for solving the problem. As you keep learning math, you keep doing more complex algorithms while solving problems.

QUESTION 61

HOW do you define a coefficient?

ANSWER > > > >

• • • • • • • • •

QUESTION 62

WHICH five symbols define inequality?

ANSWER > > > >

ANSWER 61

A coefficient is a number that is multiplied within a term that includes variables and the powers of variables. Confused? Take the term $3x^5$...in this case, 3 is the coefficient (x is the variable, and 5 is the power of the variable).

• • • • • • • • •

ANSWER 62

Any of the symbols $<$, $>$, $\leq$, or $\geq$ does the job nicely. So does $\neq$, in a different way. If you don't read hieroglyphics, they mean (in order) less than, greater than, less or equal to, greater or equal to, and not equal to. They're all equally inequal.

QUESTION 63

WHAT does it mean when an equation demonstrates the associative property?

ANSWER >>>>

· · · · · · · · · ·

QUESTION 64

WHY would you say that multiplication—but not division—is associative, also?

ANSWER >>>>

OUTSMART MATH

It means that changing the grouping of numbers in an equation does not change their value. Addition problems associate nicely, but subtraction problems do not. For example, $(2 + 3) + 4 = 2 + (3 + 4)$, but $(2 - 3) - 4 \neq 2 - (3 - 4)$.

• • • • • • • • • •

Because $2 \times (3 \times 4)$ is equal to $(2 \times 3) \times 4$. Like subtraction, however, division is not associative. $(8 \div 4) \div 2 \neq 8 \div (4 \div 2)$.

QUESTION 65

WHAT does it mean when an equation demonstrates the commutative property?

ANSWER >>>>

• • • • • • • • • •

QUESTION 66

WHAT equation shows the commutative property of addition?

ANSWER >>>>

ANSWER 65

It means that changing the order of two numbers being added (or multiplied) doesn't change the result. For example, $2 + 3 + 4 + 5 = 3 + 5 + 2 + 4$, and $2 \times 3 \times 4 \times 5 = 3 \times 5 \times 2 \times 4$.

. . . .

ANSWER 66

$a + b = b + a$ does the job nicely. By commuting, or being commutative, the terms can be reversed to get the same effect. Changing the order does not change the result.

QUESTION 67

HOW commutative is division?

ANSWER >>>>

. . . .

QUESTION 68

WHAT does it mean when an equation demonstrates the distributive property?

ANSWER >>>>

OUTSMART MATH

Not at all. Neither division nor subtraction commute. They stay home. Here's what we mean: $a - b \neq b - a$, and $a \div b \neq b \div a$ either. But multiplication commutes quickly: $a \times b = b \times a$.

• • • • • • • • •

It means that you can distribute (multiply) the number outside the parentheses by each of the terms inside the parentheses, and then add up the two products to get the same result.

QUESTION 69

HOW is the distributive property written for an addition problem?

ANSWER > > > >

· · · · · · · · · ·

QUESTION 70

WHEN an equation contains subtraction within the parentheses, can you use the distributive property to simplify?

ANSWER > > > >

ANSWER 69

$a(b + c) = ab + ac$

• • • • • • • • • •

ANSWER 70

Subtraction has excellent distributive properties. Take, for example, $a(b - c) = ab - ac$, and $2(4 - 3) = 2 \times 4 - 2 \times 3$.

QUESTION 71

WHAT about expressions containing multiplication or division? Can you use the distributive property?

ANSWER >>>>

. . . .

QUESTION 72

WHAT do you call a term that does not have a variable in it?

ANSWER >>>>

ANSWER 71

The answer is no: $a(b \times c) \neq ab \times ac$, because $2(4 \times 3) \neq (2 \times 4) \times (2 \times 3)$. The same is true with division: $a(b \div c) \neq ab \div ac$, because $2(4 \div 3) \neq 8 \div 6$.

• • • • • • • • •

ANSWER 72

That's a constant. This makes sense, because you're trying to find the opposite of a variable. 9 is a constant. So is 5.

QUESTION 73

WHAT are the three algebra terms that describe first-degree, second-degree, and third-degree polynomials?

ANSWER >>>>

• • • • • • • • • •

QUESTION 74

WHAT is the degree of a polynomial, exactly?

ANSWER >>>>

ANSWER 73

First-degree polynomials are linear. Second-degree polynomials are quadratic. Third-degree polynomials are cubic. When this comes up on the test, don't let your teacher give you the third degree. (Keep reading for some examples.)

. . . .

ANSWER 74

Remember that a polynomial is the sum of a number of monomials. The degree of a polynomial is actually the highest degree of all the monomials that are in it. (Here come those examples...)

HOW are linear (first-degree) polynomials represented?

ANSWER >>>>

• • • • • • • • • •

WHAT is a quadratic (second-degree) polynomial?

ANSWER >>>>

OUTSMART MATH

A first-degree polynomial contains a variable that's represented as a single letter with an exponent of 1. For example, x is as good a first-degree polynomial as you'll find anywhere.

. . . .

A second-degree polynomial contains a term that has an exponent of 2 on the variable, and this is the highest exponent. y^2 is perfect for the job.

QUESTION 77

HOW is a third-/fourth-/fifth- (and so on) degree polynomial represented?

ANSWER > > > >

• • • • • • • • •

QUESTION 78

WHAT is a linear equation?

ANSWER > > > >

ANSWER 77

It's a variable whose terms have an exponent represented as z^3, z^4, z^5, and so on.

· · · · · · · · ·

ANSWER 78

It's an equation that can be written with first-degree polynomials and no exponents other than 1. Here are two linear equations: $3x + 2 = 8$ and $4x + 3y = 10$.

QUESTION 79

WHAT is a quadratic equation?

ANSWER > > > >

· · · · · · · · · ·

QUESTION 80

WHAT are the first 10 numbers of the Fibonacci string or sequence?

ANSWER > > > >

ANSWER 79

A quadratic equation is an equation that has only second-degree polynomials (which contain an exponent of 2 on the variable) and lower.

• • • • • • • • • • •

ANSWER 80

To create a Fibonacci string (which is named for its creator, Leonardo Fibonacci) you start with the first two numbers, 0 and 1, and add them together to get the next number. To continue, add that number to the last number to get the next number in the string. Therefore, the first 10 numbers are 0, 1, 1, 2, 3, 5, 8, 13, 21, and 34. Why? Because 0 + 1 = 1, 1 + 1 = 2, 2 + 1 = 3, 3 + 2 = 5, 5 + 3 = 8, and so on until 13 + 21 = 34. As you probably guessed, the Fibonacci sequence is infinite.

QUESTION **81**

HOW much is a googol?

ANSWER >>>>

. . . .

QUESTION **82**

HOW many degrees are in a circle?

ANSWER >>>>

OUTSMART MATH

ANSWER 81

It is 10^{100}, or 10000000000000000000000000000
00000000000000000000000000000000000000000000
00000000000000000000000000000000000000000000.
You can look it up.

• • • • • • • • •

ANSWER 82

Ice-skaters, snowboarders, ballet dancers, and anyone else who turns in a circle for a living will tell you that every circle has 360 degrees...if they ever get around to it.

QUESTION 83

WHAT is the difference between a circle and a sphere?

ANSWER > > > >

QUESTION 84

WHAT would you call a missing parrot or a closed object with three or more line segments as sides?

ANSWER > > > >

ANSWER 83

A sphere is a three-dimensional circle, like a ball, measuring the same distance in every direction from a center point. A circle is usually two-dimensional, or flat.

• • • • • • • • • •

ANSWER 84

A polygon. (Polly-gone!) Any geometric object—from a triangle to a shape with a gazillion angles—is a polygon.

QUESTION 85

WHICH enormous government building is named for a five-sided polygon?

ANSWER > > > >

· · · · · · · · ·

QUESTION 86

WHY does the name of the six-sided polygon sound like a magic curse has worn off?

ANSWER > > > >

OUTSMART MATH

ANSWER **85**

The Pentagon. Pentagon is the name of any five-sided polygon.

● ● ● ● ● ● ● ● ●

ANSWER **86**

We don't know, but it's a hexagon.

QUESTION 87

WHAT is the geometric term for the shape of a stop sign?

ANSWER > > > >

• • • • • • • • • •

QUESTION 88

WHAT is a decagon?

ANSWER > > > >

ANSWER 87

An octagon.

ANSWER 88

A decagon is a polygon with 10 sides and 10 angles. It's bigger than a 9-sided nonagon and smaller than an 11-sided hendecagon. Twenty sides? It's an icosagon. Thirty sides? Try a triacontagon.

QUESTION 89

WHAT are parallelograms?

ANSWER > > > >

· · · · · · · · · ·

QUESTION 90

WHAT is the difference between a square and quadrilateral?

ANSWER > > > >

OUTSMART MATH

ANSWER 89

Parallelograms have four sides, and each pair of opposite lines is parallel. Squares are parallelograms. Rhombuses make fine parallelograms and so do rectangles, even though each pair of sides can be a different length.

• • • • • • • • •

ANSWER 90

A square is a quadrilateral with four equal sides and four right angles. A quadrilateral that is not a square has four sides and four angles, but the sides and the angles do not have to be equal.

QUESTION 91

WHAT is the difference between a square and a rhombus?

ANSWER > > > >

. . . .

QUESTION 92

HOW do you define a trapezoid?

ANSWER > > > >

ANSWER 91

Both shapes have four equal sides, but even though a rhombus has equal opposite angles, all four angles do not have to be equal.

● ● ● ● ● ● ● ● ●

ANSWER 92

Trapezoids have only one pair of parallel lines. The other lines can go off in any direction. A trapezoid is always a quadrilateral. For the record, the familiar trapezoid that looks like a triangle with the top point lopped off is an isosceles trapezoid.

GEOMETRY

QUESTION 93

WHICH, of a square, rhombus, quadrilateral, quadrangle, and rectangle, are always parallelograms?

ANSWER >>>>

QUESTION 94

WHAT in geometry is a plane?

ANSWER >>>>

OUTSMART MATH

ANSWER 93

Quadrangles simply have four angles. Quadrilaterals simply have four sides. A square, a rhombus, and a rectangle are quadrangles, quadrilaterals, and they are always parallelograms.

• • • • • • • • •

ANSWER 94

A plane is a two-dimensional (flat) surface stretching into infinity in all directions. Hey, lines can stretch into infinity, right? So can the polygons you create with lines. Draw a square, a triangle, or even a rhomboid trapezoid, and label the length of each side infinity, and you've just made an infinite geometric plane.

QUESTION 95

WHAT is the perimeter of an object?

ANSWER > > > >

• • • • • • • • • •

QUESTION 96

WHAT is the really-easy-we-promise formula for finding the perimeter of a triangle?

ANSWER > > > >

OUTSMART MATH

Whenever someone is guarding the perimeter of a place or an object, they're guarding all the outside edges. If that object happens to be a triangle, determining its perimeter is as easy as 1-2-3. Why? See the next question...

• • • • • • • • •

Add up the lengths of all three sides. Write down the sum. Put down your pencil. And you're done.

QUESTION **97**

WHAT is a square foot?

ANSWER > > > >

• • • • • • • • •

QUESTION **98**

WHAT is the area of a football field (in square feet) if the field is 300 feet long and 160 feet wide?

ANSWER > > > >

OUTSMART MATH

A square foot is not a reason to stay off the dance floor. It is a way to measure the dance floor. Imagine the floor tiles are a foot long on each side. What you have is a square foot: a square that's a foot long on every side. Two of those tiles together make a rectangle, right? That rectangle is two square feet, and so on.

• • • • • • • • •

The area of any parallelogram is length × width. Because the football field's length is 300 feet and the width is 160 feet, then the area is 300 × 160, or 48,000 square feet. That may sound large, but it feels small when people are chasing you and trying to tackle you.

QUESTION 99

WHAT is the simpler name for a closed curve, whose many points (all of them) are the same distance from its center?

ANSWER > > > >

• • • • • • • •

QUESTION 100

WHAT is another name for the perimeter of a circle?

ANSWER > > > >

OUTSMART MATH

The simpler name is a circle. We just rounded it out.

• • • • • • • • •

The perimeter of a circle is the circumference.

QUESTION 101

WHICH term describes a part of a circle, but not a complete circle?

ANSWER > > > >

• • • • • • • • • •

QUESTION 102

WHAT do you call the longest distance from one point to another on a circle?

ANSWER > > > >

OUTSMART MATH

ANSWER 101

Part of a circle is an arc. Picture an arc in your mind. Can you see how it would be part of a circle? The letters C and U are also good examples of arcs. (If arc sounds like three-fourths of the word arch, that's not a coincidence.)

• • • • • • • • • •

ANSWER 102

The diameter is the longest distance across a circle.

QUESTION 103

WHAT is a chord (in a circle, not in music)?

ANSWER > > > >

QUESTION 104

HOW would you slice a pizza if you were cutting along its radius?

ANSWER > > > >

OUTSMART MATH

A chord is a line segment that has both its endpoints on the circle itself. A diameter is a chord. A much smaller line, found inside the circle that has both ends touching the circle, is also a chord.

• • • • • • • • • •

You would cut the pizza from the middle to one edge—but you'd need to cut two of those radius lines to get a whole slice.

QUESTION 105

HOW would you slice a pizza if you were cutting its diameter?

ANSWER > > > >

• • • • • • • • •

QUESTION 106

WHEN you cut across your rectangular sheet pizza from one corner to the opposite corner, what is that line called?

ANSWER > > > >

OUTSMART MATH

ANSWER 105

You would cut the pizza in half through the middle.
The diameter goes through the center of a circle.
If your pizza is a rectangular sheet pizza, you are
disqualified until the next question.

• • • • • • • • • • •

ANSWER 106

It's called a diagonal. Now you have two really
large slices. Keep cutting.

QUESTION 107

WHAT (as long as we're discussing pizza with corners) is the formula for the area of a circle?

ANSWER > > > >

· · · · · · · · ·

QUESTION 108

WHAT exactly is π (pi)?

ANSWER > > > >

ANSWER 107

The area of a circle = pi × radius squared, or πr^2. Pi are squared. Get it?

• • • • • • • • •

ANSWER 108

Pi is the ratio of the circumference of a circle to its diameter. Pi is also estimated to be $\frac{22}{7}$, and that's true 24/7.

GEOMETRY

QUESTION 109

WHAT are the first three digits of π (pi)?

ANSWER > > > >

• • • • • • • • •

QUESTION 110

WHAT is a sector?

ANSWER > > > >

ANSWER **109**

They're 3.14. That's because 22 ÷ 7 = 3.14, and then some. The first 10 digits of pi, in case you're interested, are 3.141592654.

• • • • • • • • •

ANSWER **110**

A sector is a fraction of a circle. It's also the mathematical term for the shape of a slice of pizza cut from a round pie.

QUESTION 111

WHICH formula helps you calculate the circumference (or perimeter or outside edge) of a circle?

ANSWER > > > >

• • • • • • • • • •

QUESTION 112

WHICH formula helps you calculate the diameter of a circle?

ANSWER > > > >

ANSWER 111

The formula is 2 × π × radius, or $2\pi r$ if you can do the shorthand. If each side of your pizza slice (the radius) is 10 inches long, multiply 2 × 3.14 (π) × 10″. That's 6.28 × 10″, which means the circumference (or perimeter or outside edge) of the pizza is 62.8″. Hope you're hungry.

• • • • • • • • • •

ANSWER 112

This is an easy one: Use a ruler to get the widest possible measurement straight across the middle. If it's a really big circle, use a really big ruler. If you know the circumference of the circle, use the formula diameter = circumference ÷ pi, or $D = C \div \pi$.

QUESTION 113

WHAT is a geometric solid?

ANSWER > > > >

. . . .

QUESTION 114

WHERE is the base of any figure?

ANSWER > > > >

ANSWER 113

A solid is a three-dimensional shape, which means it has a length, width, and height. Isn't that a gas?

• • • • • • • • •

ANSWER 114

It's on the bottom. For example, the base of a pyramid is the side that sits on the desert floor. Circular shapes, like a sphere, don't have a base, which makes the word "baseball" impossible from a geometric viewpoint.

QUESTION 115

WHAT is the definition of a pyramid?

ANSWER > > > >

• • • • • • • • •

QUESTION 116

WHAT is a 3-D square called?

ANSWER > > > >

ANSWER 115

Here's the point: A pyramid is a 3-D figure with a polygon base and four faces. Each of the faces is a triangle. Each of the triangular faces shares a single vertex at the top point. And inside a few pyramids are untold riches, cool hieroglyphics, and dead guys wrapped in ratty bandages.

• • • • • • • • •

ANSWER 116

It's a cube, and because cubes are 3-D, they always have six sides.

QUESTION 117

HOW do you calculate the surface area of any figure with flat sides?

ANSWER > > > >

QUESTION 118

HOW do you get the surface area of a sphere?

ANSWER > > > >

OUTSMART MATH

Just add up the areas of all the faces. On a cube, that's height × width × 6. If a cube footstool is two feet long on every side, that's 2 × 2 × 6, or an area of 24 feet.

• • • • • • • • • •

Start with your formula for the area of a circle— πr^2—and multiply that by four, for a formula of $4\pi r^2$. That big beach ball you love has a radius of 10 inches, and 4 × 3.14 (π) is 12.56. Find the square of the radius, $10^2 = 100$, and multiply that by 12.56. The ball's surface area is 1,256 square inches.

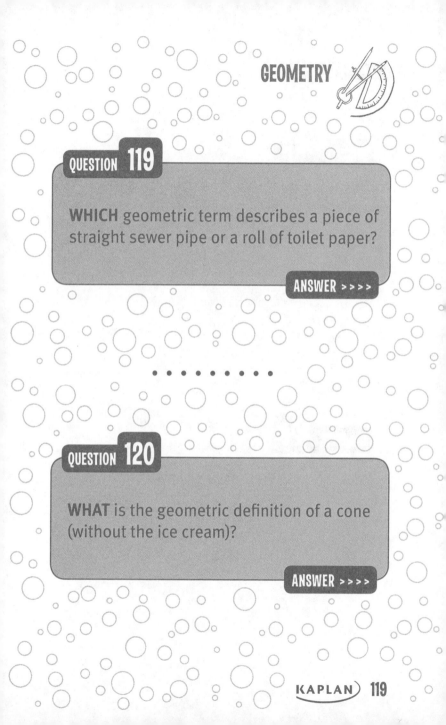

GEOMETRY

QUESTION 119

WHICH geometric term describes a piece of straight sewer pipe or a roll of toilet paper?

ANSWER >>>>

• • • • • • • • • •

QUESTION 120

WHAT is the geometric definition of a cone (without the ice cream)?

ANSWER >>>>

OUTSMART MATH

A cylinder. This is defined as a 3-D figure whose bases are two parallel circles.

• • • • • • • • •

Here's the scoop: A cone is a 3-D figure with one circular base and one vertex. Remember the vertex? That's when two lines (or rays) share a common endpoint and make an angle.

QUESTION 121

WHAT is the fancy geometric word for an oval?

ANSWER > > > >

• • • • • • • • • •

QUESTION 122

HOW do you define volume?

ANSWER > > > >

ANSWER 121

Ellipse is the fancy geometric word for oval.

• • • • • • • •

ANSWER 122

Volume is the number of cubic units needed to fill an object. The volume of a one-gallon paint can is one gallon. The volume of a 16 oz. soft drink bottle is 16 oz. The volume of a 20 oz. box of cereal is supposed to be 20 oz., but in reality, when you get home you find it's about 10 oz. of cereal and 10 oz. of air.

QUESTION 123

HOW do you calculate the area of a triangle?

ANSWER > > > >

• • • • • • • • •

QUESTION 124

WHICH shape has its own name built into the formula for finding its area?

ANSWER > > > >

OUTSMART MATH

ANSWER 123

The area of a triangle is exactly equivalent to one-half of its base times its height. In a more precise, less wordy form, the answer is also $\frac{1}{2}$ bh.

• • • • • • • • •

ANSWER 124

The good old dependable square is at the root of the simplest formulas, and the formula for finding a square's area with a side length of x is x^2. That's x squared.

QUESTION 125

WHAT is the trick for finding the volume of a solid rectangle (also known as a rectangular solid)?

ANSWER > > > >

. . . .

QUESTION 126

WHAT are some more weird-agons—with 40, 50, 60, 70, 80, 90, 100, 1,000, 10,000 sides?

ANSWER > > > >

OUTSMART MATH

Multiply height × width × depth. If that rectangular solid is 2′ × 3′ × 4′, then what you have is a 24 cubic foot rectangle.

• • • • • • • • •

40 = tetracontagon; 50 = pentacontagon; 60 = hexacontagon; 70 = heptacontagon; 80 = octacontagon; 90 = enneacontagon; 100 = hectogon; 1,000 = chiliagon; and 10,000 = myriagon.

QUESTION 127

WHY are an isosceles triangle, a square, and a standard octagonal stop sign all regular polygons, but not rectangles?

ANSWER > > > >

• • • • • • • • • •

QUESTION 128

WHAT is an absolute value?

ANSWER > > > >

ANSWER 127

Regular polygons have equal sides and equal angles. The rectangle has equal angles, but not equal sides.

• • • • • • • • •

ANSWER 128

An absolute value is a number's distance on the number line from zero. For example, the absolute value of 15 is 15. The absolute value of −15 is 15, too.

QUESTION 129

WHAT is a data set?

ANSWER > > > >

. . . .

QUESTION 130

WHAT is the average of 1, 2, 2, 3, and 92...
and why?

ANSWER > > > >

OUTSMART MATH

ANSWER 129

A data set is a collection of related data. It could be the birthdates of your classmates, a list of the number of sprinkles on 31 different ice cream cones, or even a set of arbitrary numbers such as 1, 2, 2, 3, and 92.

• • • • • • • • • •

ANSWER 130

It's 20, because the average is the result of adding up all your numbers, then dividing the total by the amount of numbers you just added. In this case, $1 + 2 + 2 + 3 + 92 = 100$, and $100 \div 5 = 20$.

QUESTION **131**

WHAT is the mean of 1, 2, 2, 3, and 92... and why?

ANSWER > > > >

• • • • • • • •

QUESTION **132**

WHAT is the median of 1, 2, 2, 3, and 92... and why?

ANSWER > > > >

OUTSMART MATH

ANSWER 131

It's 20, because the mean is just another word for the average.

• • • • • • • • •

ANSWER 132

It's 2, because the median is the middle number in a string of numbers that are arranged in order.

QUESTION 133

WHAT is the mode of 1, 2, 2, 3, and 92... and why?

ANSWER > > > >

• • • • • • • • • •

QUESTION 134

WHAT is the range of 1, 2, 2, 3, and 92... and why?

ANSWER > > > >

OUTSMART MATH

It's 2, because the mode is the number that occurs most frequently in any set of numbers.

· · · · · · · · ·

It's 91, because the range is the difference between the greatest and smallest values in a set. In this case, 92 is the greatest value and 1 is the smallest. Therefore, 92 − 1 = 91.

QUESTION 135

WHAT is the consecutive order of 1, 2, 2, 3, and 92...and why?

ANSWER > > > >

. . . .

QUESTION 136

WHAT is the minimum number in the group 1, 2, 2, 3, and 92...and why?

ANSWER > > > >

It's 1, 2, 2, 3, and 92, because consecutive numbers or events follow in a proper increasing (or decreasing) order without interruption. In this case, 92 doesn't usually follow 3, except there's nothing else in between. Had there been a 42 or a 75, either one would have been put before the 92.

• • • • • • • • •

Minimum means the smallest possible quantity. Therefore, the minimum number is 1.

QUESTION 137

WHAT is the maximum number of times one book can use 1, 2, 2, 3, and 92...and why?

ANSWER > > > >

• • • • • • • • •

QUESTION 138

WHAT is a quartile?

ANSWER > > > >

OUTSMART MATH

Maximum means the most possible times we can use 1, 2, 2, 3, and 92 without causing a riot. The answer (so far) is a maximum of nine times in one book, and that is probably a world record.

When you have a set of data (or a collection of things) that you can rank—say, test grades—then you can identify the ones at the 25 percent, 50 percent, 75 percent, and 100 percent points as quartiles. To make it easy, let's say of 100 kids, no two got the same grade. So you have all the numbers from 1–100 in your set. The kid who got a 25 is at the first (or lower) quartile. The kid who got a 75 is at the third quartile.

QUESTION 139

WHAT do you call the middle, second, or 50 percent quartile?

ANSWER > > > >

. . . .

QUESTION 140

WHAT happens when you add up two odd numbers?

ANSWER > > > >

OUTSMART MATH

ANSWER 139

That's the median, and as always, 100 percent is the top.

• • • • • • • • • •

ANSWER 140

They refuse to stay odd. In fact, 99 percent of the time plus 1 percent of the time, the sum of two odd numbers will be an even number. Isn't that odd?

QUESTION 141

WHAT are factors?

ANSWER > > > >

. . . .

QUESTION 142

HOW do you find the factors of a number?

ANSWER > > > >

ANSWER 141

Factors are what you call the integers that are multiplied together to form a product. They can also be described as the whole numbers that can be evenly divided into a larger number. (The factors of 6 are 1, 2, 3, and 6.)

· · · · · · · · ·

ANSWER 142

Find the integers that divide cleanly into the number and don't leave a remainder. For example, if you're hunting for all the factors of the number 15, you'll get 1, 3, 5, and 15.

QUESTION **143**

WHAT are the common factors of two or more numbers?

ANSWER > > > >

. . . .

QUESTION **144**

HOW do you find the greatest common factor of two (or more) numbers?

ANSWER > > > >

ANSWER 143

Pick two numbers—any two numbers. Let's pick 12 and 20. Okay. The factors of 12 are 1, 2, 3, 4, 6, and 12. The factors of 20 are 1, 2, 4, 5, 10, and 20. The common factors of 12 and 20 are the factors they both share: 1, 2, and 4.

• • • • • • • • • •

ANSWER 144

Once you know the common factors, you're almost there. The largest factor shared by your numbers is the greatest common factor. With 12 and 20, the greatest common factor is 4. You can also say it's the largest number that divides evenly into two or more numbers.

QUESTION 145

WHAT are all the factors of the dimensions of an 8" × 10" glossy photograph?

ANSWER > > > >

• • • • • • • • • •

QUESTION 146

WHAT, speaking of common things, is a common multiple?

ANSWER > > > >

ANSWER 145

The dimensions are 8 and 10. Their common factors are 1 and 2. Their greatest common factor is 2. And that's a fact.

• • • • • • • • • •

ANSWER 146

A common multiple is a multiple shared by two or more numbers. Common multiples of 3 and 4 are 0, 12, 24, 36, and so on, because with those numbers, 3 and 4 each divide into them evenly. Zero is a multiple, and a common multiple, of every number.

QUESTION 147

WHAT is the least common multiple (LCM) of a number?

ANSWER > > > >

• • • • • • • • • •

QUESTION 148

HOW do you calculate the greatest common divisor (GCD) of a number?

ANSWER > > > >

OUTSMART MATH

You were going to say zero, right? Wrong. Mathematicians don't make things that easy. The least common multiple of a number is the lowest nonzero multiple. With 3 and 4, the LCM is 12.

Common divisors aren't any different than common factors. The GCD is the greatest divisor common to two (or more) numbers, while leaving a whole number after dividing. It's handy for reducing fractions to the bare bones. For example, the fraction $\frac{40}{50}$ reduces to $\frac{4}{5}$, because you can divide both numbers by 10.

QUESTION 149

HOW do you reduce a fraction?

ANSWER > > > >

• • • • • • • • •

QUESTION 150

WHAT does a decimal point do?

ANSWER > > > >

OUTSMART MATH

ANSWER 149

You can reduce or simplify a fraction to its lowest terms by dividing the numerator and denominator by their greatest common factor. With $\frac{20}{80}$, both 20 and 80 share the factor 20, which is as great as 20 can get. Dividing both by 20 gives you $\frac{1}{4}$.

• • • • • • • • •

ANSWER 150

Besides being the smallest symbol in math, the decimal's main job is to separate the whole numbers from the fractional numbers. Dot's interesting.

QUESTION 151

WHEN a number is called a decimal number, what is it?

ANSWER > > > >

. . . .

QUESTION 152

WHAT handy round number is every decimal number based on?

ANSWER > > > >

OUTSMART MATH

ANSWER 151

It's a number that has a decimal point in it. It could be a fractional number (0.15), or it could be a mixed number (1.5), too.

. . . .

ANSWER 152

Every decimal number is based on a power of 10. The decimal number 0.2 is the same as the fractions $\frac{2}{10}$, $\frac{20}{100}$, or $\frac{200}{1,000}$. In fact, the word decimal shares the same dec- prefix as decade (10 years), decathlon (10 athletic events), and December (which, in ancient times, used to be the 10th month).

QUESTION 153

WHEN converting fractions to decimals, what's interesting about $\frac{1}{2}$ and $\frac{1}{5}$?

ANSWER >>>>

. . . .

QUESTION 154

WHAT happens to the fraction $\frac{1}{3}$ when it's converted to a decimal number?

ANSWER >>>>

ANSWER 153

They switch off: $\frac{1}{2}$ converts to 0.5, and $\frac{1}{5}$ converts to 0.2.

• • • • • • • • •

ANSWER 154

It heads off into infinity. $\frac{1}{3}$ becomes 0.3333333333
333333333333333333333333333333333333333
333333333333333333333333333333333333333
333333333333333333333333333333333333333
3333333333333333333333333333333333333333
and never ends.

QUESTION 155

WHAT is a repeating decimal?

ANSWER > > > >

• • • • • • • • •

QUESTION 156

WHAT is a terminating decimal?

ANSWER > > > >

ANSWER 155

It's a decimal whose digits repeat endlessly.
Like $\frac{1}{3}$ equaling 0.33333333...or $\frac{2}{11}$ equaling
0.181818181818...or $\frac{89}{44}$, which equals
2.0227272727272727272727272...

• • • • • • • • •

ANSWER 156

Terminating decimals do not go on forever. They
terminate (or stop) and usually stop pretty quickly.
You might think $\frac{8}{5}$ would yield a good repeating
decimal, stretching across the page, but it converts
to a ho-hum 1.6—a terminating decimal.

QUESTION 157

WHAT is probability?

ANSWER >>>>

· · · · · · · · · ·

QUESTION 158

HOW do you determine probability?

ANSWER >>>>

OUTSMART MATH

Probability is a measure used in experiments to determine the number of times that an outcome is likely to happen (such as a dropped slice of buttered toast landing butter-side-down and buttering the carpet). Probability takes into account the number of times the outcome has the chance of happening. Probability is always expressed as a ratio.

• • • • • • • • •

ANSWER 158

Probability is actually fairly simple to determine. The number of possible outcomes (100 dropped slices of buttered toast) is the denominator. The number of successful outcomes (50 fuzzy, butter-down slices of toast) is the numerator. Therefore, the probability at our house was 50 out of 100. Does that make us butterfingers?

QUESTION 159

HOW can probability be defined as a ratio?

ANSWER > > > >

• • • • • • • • •

QUESTION 160

WHAT is the probability that, all things being equal, a slice of toast will land butter-side-down on the next drop?

ANSWER > > > >

OUTSMART MATH

As you recall, the probability of the butter hitting the rug at our house was 50 out of 100; $\frac{50}{100} = \frac{1}{2} =$ 1:2 = a 1 in 2 chance of butter hitting the rug. Your results may vary.

• • • • • • • • • •

We'll presume that you have a two-sided slice of toast. We'll presume you only buttered one side of it, and we'll presume you have a flat floor in a room where gravity is in normal mode. With all of that taken into consideration, the odds are exactly the same as a coin landing heads or tails: 50 percent, or 1 in 2.

QUESTION 161

WHAT is the probability that, after the toast lands nine times in a row butter-side-down, the 10th drop will be butter-side-down?

ANSWER >>>>

. . . .

QUESTION 162

HOW can probability be expressed when something is nine times more likely to happen than not?

ANSWER >>>>

ANSWER 161

It's still $\frac{50}{100}$, 1 in 2, 50 percent, or even odds. This is because no matter what has happened before, if all factors remain unchanged (say, the accumulated rug fuzz doesn't influence things), the original probability (in this case, $\frac{50}{100}$) always stays the same as it ever was.

• • • • • • • • •

ANSWER 162

Let's say you are on the varsity tee-ball team. Your chances at bat are pretty good—since you were a little kid, you hit the ball 90 percent of the time. So the probability today is that 9 times out of 10, you're going to hit the ball off its tee. Therefore, your chances are 9 to 1, or 9:1, meaning before you even get up to bat, you're nine times likelier to hit than whiff.

QUESTION **163**

HOW do you compare ratios to determine which one is greater?

ANSWER > > > >

· · · · · · · · · ·

QUESTION **164**

HOW do you define a proportion?

ANSWER > > > >

OUTSMART MATH

One way is to convert them to fractions and simplify to a common denominator. For example, 8:10 and 2:5 become $\frac{8}{10}$ and $\frac{2}{5}$, which reduce (or simplify) to $\frac{4}{5}$ and $\frac{2}{5}$.

• • • • • • • • • •

Proportions are equations with a ratio on each side. Proportions state that the two ratios are equal. An example of a proportion is $\frac{2}{3} = \frac{4}{6}$.

QUESTION 165

HOW does cross-multiplication work?

ANSWER > > > >

• • • • • • • • •

QUESTION 166

WHAT do you do when one of a proportion's four numbers is a question mark or variable?

ANSWER > > > >

OUTSMART MATH

When you have two fractions that are set equal to each other, you can multiply each numerator by the opposite denominator to find your answer. For example, you start with $\frac{a}{b} = \frac{c}{d}$. Then you multiply ad and bc. The product should be the same. Now add numbers: $\frac{2}{3} = \frac{4}{6}$ ...2 × 6 = 12 and 3 × 4 = 12. Voila!

• • • • • • • • • •

You solve the proportion. How? By cross-multiplying: $\frac{2}{3} : \frac{x}{6}$ becomes 2 × 6 = 3x, which becomes 12 = 3x, which makes $x = 4$. Now that you've found the missing number, it fits in the original proportion as $\frac{2}{3} = \frac{4}{6}$.

QUESTION 167

WHAT is a rate?

ANSWER >>>>

• • • • • • • • • •

QUESTION 168

HOW do you express rates as ratios and fractions?

ANSWER >>>>

OUTSMART MATH

ANSWER 167

Rates are ratios that show how long it takes to do something. Running 20 miles in an hour makes your rate 20 miles per hour (or 20 mph). Picking 300 boysenberries an hour puts you at the rate of 300 bph.

ANSWER 168

The quantity of berries picked, miles run, or other feats of amazement are expressed as numerators. The units of time you spent are expressed as denominators. Therefore, 300 berries per hour is 300:1, or $\frac{300}{1}$. If you spend four hours picking 1,200 berries, then your ratio is $\frac{1,200}{4}$, or 1,200:4, and still 300 bph (and your hands are bright blue).

QUESTION **169**

HOW do you determine your average rate of speed?

ANSWER > > > >

• • • • • • • • • •

QUESTION **170**

WHAT is a fun yet informative example that quickly explains the rate of speed?

ANSWER > > > >

OUTSMART MATH

ANSWER **169**

Your average rate of speed depends on three things: your sneakers, your tires, and most importantly, this ratio: the total distance traveled divided by the total time of your trip. Please read on for a fun yet informative example that quickly explains the rate of speed.

• • • • • • • • • •

ANSWER **170**

Here's one! You sing the Bulgarian national anthem (it's not your native tongue) at the rate of two words per minute. The second time you sing faster (and more clearly) at four words per minute. Comparing two and four, you get an average rate of speed of three words per minute. Which, again, isn't bad for a language you don't understand.

QUESTION **171**

HOW do you write the fun yet informative example in the previous question as an equation?

ANSWER > > > >

. . . .

QUESTION **172**

WHAT is the probability of picking (blindfolded) a moldy peach from a bin of 84 peaches if you know 63 of them are rotten?

ANSWER > > > >

OUTSMART MATH

ANSWER 171

The equation is: 2 wpm (words per minute) +
4 wpm = 6 wpm. The average is 6 ÷ 2 = 3 wpm.
You can count on it.

• • • • • • • • • • •

ANSWER 172

If you said 63 out of 84, or 3 out of 4, you'd be
right. But smart Outsmart readers would say 0 out
of 84, because they never would have stuck their
hands into that nasty bin.

QUESTION 173

HOW do you compare rates to determine who picked more apples?

ANSWER >>>>

• • • • • • • • •

QUESTION 174

WHICH kind of number is zero: positive or negative?

ANSWER >>>>

ANSWER 173

It's much like comparing ratios. By converting the denominators to a common number, regardless of what the units are, you'll have your answer. As long as you're comparing similar units of time and other quantities, it's like comparing apples and apples.

• • • • • • • • •

ANSWER 174

Zero is neither negative nor positive. It's very even-tempered, and it is in fact an even number. Zero has no size, no quantity, and no magnitude— and it's a very cold temperature.

QUESTION 175

WHY is zero a number if it doesn't do anything?

ANSWER >>>>

• • • • • • • •

QUESTION 176

HOW can you use the number zero to help you make up stories without actually lying?

ANSWER >>>>

OUTSMART MATH

Zero does a lot, actually, even though some
dictionaries define it as having no importance.
For instance, zero causes other numbers not to
change during addition and subtraction. It reflects
the arrival of a new decimal place (and new decade
and new millennium). It's the number that registers
a reading of zero on a scale or thermometer. It also
keeps 1 and −1 apart.

• • • • • • • • •

You can tell people you have been in a number
of Hollywood films or you can juggle a number
of porcupines behind your back and not be lying.
However, if they ask, you must tell them the
number you're talking about is zero.

QUESTION **177**

HOW many digits are there—a finite amount or an infinite amount?

ANSWER > > > >

• • • • • • • • •

QUESTION **178**

HOW many digits are in 1,040?

ANSWER > > > >

OUTSMART MATH

ANSWER 177

There are a very, very, very, very finite amount of digits. There are 10, actually, just as there are 26 letters. The digits run from 0 to 9. Sometimes they're called symbols. Dig it?

• • • • • • • • •

ANSWER 178

There are four. The 1, the 0, the 4, and the other 0 are each digits. Why are they called digits? The answer is at your fingertips—because humans count best when they're counting on their fingers, and fingers are the original digits.

QUESTION 179

WHAT is a positive number?

ANSWER >>>>

. . . .

QUESTION 180

WHAT, officially, is a negative number, and what are some positive uses of them?

ANSWER >>>>

ANSWER 179

A positive number is any number that is greater than zero. Therefore, 0.0000000000000000001 is a positive number—a very small positive number.

. . . .

ANSWER 180

A negative number is any number that is less than zero. Some positive uses of negative numbers include debt (your bank balance can be −$100) and very low temperatures (−30 degrees). Come to think of it, those examples aren't so positive after all.

QUESTION 181

WHAT is an integer?

ANSWER > > > >

. . . .

QUESTION 182

WHAT is a nonnegative integer?

ANSWER > > > >

OUTSMART MATH

ANSWER **181**

Integers are all the whole numbers: the positive (1, 2, 3...), the negative (...–3, –2, –1), and zero (0).

• • • • • • • • •

ANSWER **182**

A nonnegative integer is just like a positive integer, except the nonnegative integer also includes zero (0, 1, 2, 3...). This may sound like splitting hairs to you, but the zero fought long and hard to get included on that list.

QUESTION 183

WHAT is the more natural name for a nonnegative integer?

ANSWER > > > >

• • • • • • • • •

QUESTION 184

WHAT is the difference between a nonpositive integer and a negative integer?

ANSWER > > > >

OUTSMART MATH

ANSWER 183

A natural number. Sometimes they're called the counting numbers. Naturally.

• • • • • • • • •

ANSWER 184

A nonpositive integer is just like a negative integer, but with the zero included. Zero seems to be getting a lot of special treatment around here lately.

QUESTION 185

WHAT, if you're in your mathematical prime, is a prime number?

ANSWER > > > >

• • • • • • • • •

QUESTION 186

WHAT is the sum of the first five prime numbers?

ANSWER > > > >

OUTSMART MATH

An integer greater than one is called a prime number if it can only be divided by one and itself without leaving a remainder.

• • • • • • • • • •

The first five prime numbers are 2, 3, 5, 7, and 11. Add 'em up and you get 28.

QUESTION 187

WHAT is a rational number?

ANSWER > > > >

• • • • • • • • •

QUESTION 188

WHICH word is used to define the relationship between the two numbers in a fraction?

ANSWER > > > >

OUTSMART MATH

ANSWER 187

It is another name for a fraction. Isn't that reasonable?

. . . .

ANSWER 188

A ratio is the relationship of some measure between two different things, like the numbers in a fraction. Here's an example. Four hotdogs divided by five people equals four complete hotdog eaters and one hungry person. The result is the ratio of 4 to 5.

QUESTION 189

WHAT does percent mean?

ANSWER >>>>

• • • • • • • • • •

QUESTION 190

WHAT is another, more quotable name for the result you get when dividing the values in a ratio or fraction?

ANSWER >>>>

OUTSMART MATH

ANSWER 189

It is a fraction (or ratio) with the denominator equal to 100. (Per cent means per hundred.) Any number shown as a percentage is therefore divided by 100. $\frac{1}{100}$ is 1 percent. $\frac{43}{100}$ is 43 percent. $\frac{303}{100}$ is 303 percent. Here's something you may not know: If you put the two little zeros in the % sign to the right of the little slash (also called a vinculum), then you have /00, or 100.

• • • • • • • • •

ANSWER 190

It's a quotient—and did you realize that by adding *f*, *c*, and *n* to the word ratio you get the word fraction?

QUESTION 191

WHY are irrational numbers named as such?

ANSWER >>>>

· · · · · · · · · ·

QUESTION 192

WHAT is a square root?

ANSWER >>>>

OUTSMART MATH

Irrational numbers are real numbers that can't be expressed as a fraction or ratio. (The word irrational literally means "can't make a ratio.") An example of an irrational number is the square root of 2. If you tried to figure out the square root of 2, you would get a string of numbers that went on infinitely. Now that's irrational.

. . . .

Square roots are not what grow at the bottom of math trees. The square root of a number is a smaller number that, when squared, becomes the original number. The square root of 9 is 3, because 3^2 (three squared) is 9. The square root of 16 is 4, because 4×4 is 16. Square roots are written as a symbol like this: $\sqrt{16}$.

QUESTION 193

WHAT is the symbol $\sqrt{}$ called in a square root expression?

ANSWER > > > >

• • • • • • • • •

QUESTION 194

WHAT, without using a pencil (if you can), are the square roots of 0.04, 0.09, and 0.16?

ANSWER > > > >

OUTSMART MATH

ANSWER 193

It's called a radical. Totally.

• • • • • • • • •

ANSWER 194

0.2, 0.3, and 0.4. It's just the same as if you were doing regular square roots, but with decimals. 0.2 × 0.2 = 0.04 (move those decimals!), 0.3 × 0.3 = 0.09, and 0.4 × 0.4 = 0.16.

QUESTION **195**

WHAT kind of number is a real number?

ANSWER > > > >

• • • • • • • • •

QUESTION **196**

WHAT are imaginary numbers, and what real letter is used to represent them?

ANSWER > > > >

OUTSMART MATH

A real number is just about any kind of number there is—rational and irrational. The only kind of numbers that aren't real numbers are the kind called imaginary numbers.

• • • • • • • • • •

If you believe in imaginary numbers, clap your hands. An imaginary number is usually portrayed as the letter *i*, and it equals the square root of –1. "Aha!" you say. "There is no square root of –1." You're right, but *i* makes it possible for the math-minded to figure out the square root of any other negative number—which also can't really exist, but mathematicians thought it would be handy to know these imaginary answers anyway.

QUESTION 197

HOW do you define $\frac{1}{3}$, $\frac{2}{6}$, $\frac{3}{9}$, and $\frac{4}{12}$ exactly...as four rational numbers, or just one?

ANSWER > > > >

. . . .

QUESTION 198

WHICH number in a fraction is the numerator, and what is its job?

ANSWER > > > >

OUTSMART MATH

Each of those fractions is but a single rational number, whose simplest form is $\frac{1}{3}$. Now, isn't that rational?

The number that's on top is the numerator. It represents how many parts of the whole are being described. In the ratio $\frac{5}{17}$, we are describing 5 slices of a 17-slice pizza, and 5 is the numerator.

QUESTION 199

WHAT is the main purpose of a denominator?

ANSWER > > > >

. . . .

QUESTION 200

WHEN would a denominator be called common?

ANSWER > > > >

OUTSMART MATH

The denominator, which is the number on the bottom of a fraction, represents the number of parts that make up the whole. Remember that 17-slice pizza? In this case, the denominator is 17, because 17 slices make up the whole pizza.

• • • • • • • • • •

It's a common denominator when it is a whole number (except zero) that is divisible by all the denominators you're comparing. For example, the fractions $\frac{1}{2}$, $\frac{1}{4}$, and $\frac{1}{8}$ all have a common denominator of 8, 16, or 24 (among other multiples of 8) because 8, 16, and 24 are divisible by 2, 4, and 8.

QUESTION 201

WHEN is a denominator the least common denominator?

ANSWER > > > >

· · · · · · · · · ·

QUESTION 202

WHAT is the difference between a denominator and a divisor?

ANSWER > > > >

OUTSMART MATH

ANSWER 201

The least common denominator is the least common multiple of the denominator. The least common denominator of $\frac{1}{2}$, $\frac{1}{4}$, and $\frac{1}{8}$ is 8.

• • • • • • • • •

ANSWER 202

The difference is the spelling. Otherwise, they both represent the amount being divided in a fraction or division problem.

QUESTION 203

WHAT is the difference between a difference and a divisor?

ANSWER >>>>

. . . .

QUESTION 204

WHAT is a multiple?

ANSWER >>>>

ANSWER 203

A difference is the result of subtracting numbers.
In the equation 3 − 2 = 1, 1 is the difference.
A divisor is an integer that divides a number.
In the equation 8 ÷ 4 = 2, 4 is the divisor.

• • • • • • • • • •

ANSWER 204

A multiple is what you get when you multiply
any integer (say, 3) by any whole number
(0, 1, 2, 3, etc.). The result: 0, 3, 6, 9, and
so on are all multiples of 3.

6

QUESTION 205

WHAT is a product?

ANSWER >>>>

• • • • • • • • •

QUESTION 206

WHAT is $\frac{1}{2}$ of $\frac{1}{4}$ of $\frac{1}{8}$?

ANSWER >>>>

OUTSMART MATH

If you are in the ship-in-a-bottle business, your product is small, hard-to-build ships. If you're in the math business, the product is what you get when you multiply integers together. The product of 4 and 5 is 20.

• • • • • • • • •

$\frac{1}{64}$. In order to answer a question like this one, just multiply the numerators by the numerators, and the denominators by the denominators.

QUESTION 207

WHAT is the reciprocal of $\frac{1}{2}$?

ANSWER >>>>

• • • • • • • • •

QUESTION 208

HOW do you divide a number by a fraction?

ANSWER >>>>

ANSWER 207

2. Or, more precisely, $\frac{2}{1}$. The reciprocal of a fraction is the fraction turned upside down. The purpose of this is to create a number that will equal one when it's multiplied by the original fraction. $\frac{1}{2} \times \frac{2}{1}$ (or 2) = 1. Also, $\frac{4}{5} \times \frac{5}{4} = 1$, and yes, $\frac{3}{17} \times \frac{17}{3} = 1$.

• • • • • • • • •

ANSWER 208

You flip the fraction over (making the reciprocal) and multiply. For example, 10 divided by $\frac{1}{2}$ is the same as $10 \times \frac{2}{1}$, which equals 10×2, which equals 20.

QUESTION 209

HOW do you divide a fraction by a fraction?

ANSWER > > > >

. . . .

QUESTION 210

WHAT is an improper fraction?

ANSWER > > > >

ANSWER 209

The same way you divide a number by a fraction. You flip over (or take the reciprocal of) the second fraction and multiply. $\frac{1}{2}$ divided by $\frac{1}{2}$ is the same as $\frac{1}{2} \times \frac{2}{1}$, or $\frac{1}{2} \times 2$.

• • • • • • • • • •

ANSWER 210

We're sorry to report that improper fractions sound like more fun than they really are. When the numerator is greater than the denominator (such as $\frac{2}{1}$ or $\frac{4,302}{2,151}$), then a fraction is improper.

QUESTION 211

WHY are mixed numbers mixed?

ANSWER > > > >

. . . .

QUESTION 212

HOW do you turn a mixed number into an improper fraction?

ANSWER > > > >

OUTSMART MATH

They're not confused. Mixed numbers are just whole numbers and fractions combined, like $2\frac{3}{4}$. Mixed numbers also spend some time being improper.

• • • • • • • • •

Some want to be mixed. Others want to be improper. Convert your mixed number by multiplying your big whole number by your dainty denominator and then adding the result to the numerator. For instance, $2\frac{3}{4}$ becomes the improper fraction $\frac{11}{4}$ by following that procedure. $2 \times 4 = 8$ and $8 + 3 = 11$. Likewise, the mixed number $3\frac{2}{3}$ doubles as $\frac{11}{3}$, because $3 \times 3 = 9$ and $9 + 2 = 11$.

QUESTION 213

HOW do you multiply two mixed numbers?

ANSWER > > > >

. . . .

QUESTION 214

WHAT is the ratio of kids let loose in an electronics store to $2 CDs if there are 1,500 kids and three CDs left?

ANSWER > > > >

OUTSMART MATH

ANSWER 213

You turn them each into their improper fraction form, multiply the fractions, and if you really feel like it, turn the result back into a mixed number.

• • • • • • • • •

ANSWER 214

The ratio is 1,500:3, or 500:1, or $\frac{3}{1,500}$, or $\frac{1}{500}$, or 0.002. Very, very unlikely would be the way to express your odds of getting your hands on those CDs.

QUESTION **215**

WHAT is the sixth root of 64?

ANSWER > > > >

. . . .

QUESTION **216**

WHAT exactly is a graph?

ANSWER > > > >

OUTSMART MATH

2. Because 2 × 2 × 2 × 2 × 2 × 2 = 64. While we're at it, the sixth power of 2 is 64.

• • • • • • • • • •

A graph is a drawing, diagram, or some other kind of visual used to organize data and make it easier to understand. These diagrams show the relationship between sets of numbers.

QUESTION 217

WHAT do lines, bars, and pies all have in common?

ANSWER > > > >

· · · · · · · · · ·

QUESTION 218

WHEN do you use a bar graph?

ANSWER > > > >

OUTSMART MATH

ANSWER **217**

They're all kinds of graphs. Lines are (mainly) horizontal, bars are (mainly) vertical, and pies are (mainly) round—and delicious.

ANSWER **218**

Bar graphs show relationships and differences between groups. The items being compared don't have to affect each other. Imagine one book gets a two-star rating, another gets a four-star rating, and the last book gets a five-star rating. (That's this book!) If you line up each book's stars in parallel columns, you have a bar graph that looks like a staircase. Now you can quickly see the highest-rated book or whatever other differences you're measuring.

218

WHEN do you use a pie graph (also called a circle graph)?

ANSWER >>>>

. . . .

WHEN do you use a line graph?

ANSWER >>>>

OUTSMART MATH

Circle graphs are handy to show the parts, percentages, or fractions of something whole. The circle is the whole; each wedge is a part. How many kids in your school are blond? Brown-haired? Redheaded? The total number of kids is your circle. Each hair type is a wedge in the circle. The more redheaded kids you have, the bigger the redhead wedge.

. . . .

Line graphs will show data that continue over time, as one thing affects another. That zigzag pulse line your heart doctor looks at: a line graph. That zigzag line that shows how a company is losing money over time: a line graph. The letter X can form in a line graph, too. Say your grades start at the bottom left and go up to the top right; your friend's grades start at the top and plummet to the bottom right over the same time. See the X? The facts don't lie.

CHARTS & GRAPHS

QUESTION 221

WHAT is an axis?

ANSWER > > > >

• • • • • • • • • •

QUESTION 222

WHAT does horizontal mean?

ANSWER > > > >

OUTSMART MATH

ANSWER 221

Line graphs are plotted along two lines: a horizontal line and a vertical line. Each line is an axis. Using the two axes (pronounced AX-eez) on a graph, you can determine the position of one or more points.

. . . .

ANSWER 222

It means flat across, like a horizon, or a road, or a person lying in bed who has a headache from too many math questions.

QUESTION 223

WHAT does vertical mean?

ANSWER > > > >

• • • • • • • • • •

QUESTION 224

WHAT is the horizontal axis called, and what does it usually measure?

ANSWER > > > >

OUTSMART MATH

ANSWER 223

It means up and down, like a flagpole, or a skyscraper, or a person standing in a cold shower trying to wake up from the nap that was inspired by too many math questions.

· · · · · · · · · ·

ANSWER 224

The horizontal axis is the *x*-axis. It generally measures the passage of time. The more time you measure on a line graph, the farther to the right the point goes.

QUESTION 225

WHAT is the slope of a perfectly horizontal line running along the *x*-axis?

ANSWER >>>>

. . . .

QUESTION 226

WHAT is the *x*-intercept?

ANSWER >>>>

OUTSMART MATH

ANSWER **225**

A perfectly horizontal line has a slope of zero. Why? Because like any flat, horizontal object, it doesn't have any steepness. Remember, a line's steepness is the line's slope—and a line with no steepness has zero slope.

• • • • • • • • •

ANSWER **226**

Draw a line on your graph. See the point where your line crosses the x-axis? That represents the x-intercept.

QUESTION 227

WHAT is the vertical axis called, and what does it usually measure?

ANSWER > > > >

• • • • • • • • •

QUESTION 228

WHAT is the slope of a perfectly vertical line running on or parallel to the *y*-axis?

ANSWER > > > >

ANSWER 227

The vertical axis is the *y*-axis. It generally measures a quantity. The more you have, the higher the point goes on the line graph.

• • • • • • • • •

ANSWER 228

You may have been tempted to say 90 degrees, but resist temptation. The fact is, on a perfectly vertical line you can't define the slope. A slope needs to spread out somewhat horizontally to be measured.

QUESTION 229

WHAT is the *y*-intercept?

ANSWER >>>>

• • • • • • • • • •

QUESTION 230

WHAT do you call the location in the bottom left corner of your line graph where the *x*-axis and *y*-axis cross each other?

ANSWER >>>>

OUTSMART MATH

ANSWER 229

Go back four pages and replace each *x* with a *y*.
There's your answer.

• • • • • • • • •

ANSWER 230

In the beginning, it was called the origin.
It's the point where the *x*-axis and the *y*-axis
both register as zero. All line graphs take off
from the point of origin.

QUESTION 231

WHAT happens when you identify a value on your *x*-axis and another value on your *y*-axis?

ANSWER >>>>

. . . .

QUESTION 232

WHAT on a line graph are the coordinates of a point?

ANSWER >>>>

OUTSMART MATH

ANSWER 231

You're on your way to making a graph. You have identified two pieces of data, each with its own value. Next step: Find the point that contains those two values.

• • • • • • • • •

ANSWER 232

When you coordinate (as a verb) you bring things together. When you find a place on a line graph where the data on your x-axis and your y-axis cross lines and come together, you have a point you can put on your graph. That point you made is at the coordinates (as a noun) of the point. Each point is determined by a pair of numbers, called...you guessed it...the coordinates.

QUESTION 233

WHAT is the official verb for making a graph?

ANSWER > > > >

. . . .

QUESTION 234

WHICH number comes first when you specify your coordinates: the *x* or the *y*?

ANSWER > > > >

OUTSMART MATH

ANSWER 233

First you collect the data or coordinates, and then you plot a graph. If you use a thick pen, the plot thickens.

. . . .

ANSWER 234

Alphabetical order, numerical order—it's all the same. When a graph says a point is at (2,3), that means 2 across (on the *x*-axis) and 3 up (on the *y*-axis).

QUESTION 235

WHAT do the numbers (3,3) and (5,5) represent on a graph?

ANSWER > > > >

• • • • • • • • • •

QUESTION 236

WHAT happens when lines (or anything else) intersect?

ANSWER > > > >

OUTSMART MATH

ANSWER 235

They show that you have two coordinates on your graph. The first coordinate (3,3) is three points to the right of zero on the *x*-axis and three points to the north of zero on the *y*-axis. These coordinates are directly northeast of zero. The second point (5,5) is five points to the right of zero on the *x*-axis and five points to the north of zero on the *y*-axis. These coordinates are also directly northeast of zero. Draw a line between the points and the origin (0,0), and you have a line that perfectly bisects your axes at a 45-degree angle.

· · · · · · · · · ·

ANSWER 236

They come together. When lines intersect on a graph, you get a point. When roads come together, it's an intersection. When cars come together at an intersection, one of them had better stop.

QUESTION **237**

WHAT is a transversal?

ANSWER > > > >

• • • • • • • • •

QUESTION **238**

WHAT are Cartesian coordinates?

ANSWER > > > >

OUTSMART MATH

That's a line that intersects two other lines. Often, transversals cut across parallel lines— and when cars cut across parallel lines, one of them had really better stop.

. . . .

That's the official name for the pair of numbers used to identify two points on a plane: *x* first, *y* second.

QUESTION 239

WHAT is the coordinate plane?

ANSWER > > > >

. . . .

QUESTION 240

WHAT do you call each of the sections of a coordinate plane line graph?

ANSWER > > > >

ANSWER 239

It's another name for a graph with the *x*-axis and *y*-axis crossing in the center (like a plus sign), rather than just at a single right angle (like an L). Coordinate plane graphs are divided into four sections in order to represent every possible combination—both positive and negative—of *x*- and *y*-values.

• • • • • • • • •

ANSWER 240

They are quadrants. Quad = 4.

QUESTION 241

WHICH direction do you move in when you're counting a coordinate plane graph's four quadrants—clockwise or counterclockwise?

ANSWER >>>>

· · · · · · · · · ·

QUESTION 242

WHAT is true of any points south of the x-axis and west of the y-axis on a coordinate plane graph?

ANSWER >>>>

OUTSMART MATH

ANSWER 241

Quadrants are counted counterclockwise.
The first quadrant is top right. The second is top
left. The third is bottom left. The fourth quadrant
is bottom right.

. . . .

ANSWER 242

Those points represent negative numbers.
Only a point in the top right quadrant is 100
percent positive. Every point south of the *x*-axis
has a negative *x*-value, and every point west of
the *y*-axis has a negative *y*-value. Way down in the
bottom left quadrant, both values are negative.

QUESTION 243

WHAT is the formula for the slope of a line?

ANSWER >>>>

QUESTION 244

WHAT is the point-slope formula?

ANSWER >>>>

ANSWER 243

If you have two points, (x_1, y_1) and (x_2, y_2), then the slope $= \dfrac{y_1 - y_2}{x_1 - x_2}$.

· · · · · · · · · ·

ANSWER 244

To create the point-slope formula, you need to have the slope of the line and one point (x_1, y_1). Then you plug the numbers into the following equation: $(y - y_1) = \text{slope}\,(x - x_1)$.

WHY do you use a point-slope formula?

ANSWER > > > >

. . . .

WHAT shape does a linear function take?

ANSWER > > > >

OUTSMART MATH

ANSWER 245

The point-slope formula determines the equation for a line. Once you know the line's slope and one point on the line, you're right on the line.

• • • • • • • • • •

ANSWER 246

It takes the shape of a straight line. A linear function is a set of coordinates on a graph that make up a line with a constant slope...and that's why the line is totally straight when you connect the dots.

QUESTION 247

WHAT is a function?

ANSWER > > > >

. . . .

QUESTION 248

WHAT do you call a function that doesn't make a straight line (when graphed)?

ANSWER > > > >

ANSWER 247

A function is an expression involving one (or more) variables where every x-value has a unique y-value. $y = 2x$ is a function. $y = 2x - b$ is also a function. $y = ax - b$ is also, also a function.

ANSWER 248

It's a nonlinear function. Its coordinates could be all over the place. The holes in a sheet of notebook paper are linear, meaning they line up in a straight line. The holes in a piece of Swiss cheese are nonlinear.

CHARTS & GRAPHS

QUESTION 249

WHAT are the values of the four points on the coordinate plane whose coordinates contain a pair of twos?

ANSWER >>>>

• • • • • • • • •

QUESTION 250

HOW would daily high temperatures be plotted on a line graph over one week in summer?

ANSWER >>>>

OUTSMART MATH

ANSWER 249

Starting at the top right, the coordinates are (2,2).
Moving counterclockwise, in the top left, (–2,2).
Next, in the bottom left, they are (–2,–2). Finally, in
the bottom right, the coordinates are (2,–2). It's too,
too much.

● ● ● ● ● ● ● ● ●

ANSWER 250

The days of the week ride along the *x*-axis. The temperatures
rise along the *y*-axis. The high temperatures are: Monday
77 degrees, Tuesday 76 degrees, Wednesday 75 degrees,
Thursday 74 degrees, Friday 73 degrees, Saturday 72 degrees,
and Sunday 71 degrees. Each day would be a dot one point
farther to the right along the *x*-axis, and—starting at 77
degrees—each temperature would be one point lower on the
y-axis, moving to the right. Connect the dots. What you have
is a diagonal downward slope, heading southeast.

CONGRATULATIONS!

Now you're 250 times smarter than ever before. Don't forget to celebrate! Once you're done with your victory dance, here are some other ways to use this book:

- Show the world how wise you are. Take your favorite *Outsmart* trivia tidbits, and drop them into everyday conversation.

- Have an *Outsmart* party! Invite some friends over. Find some math-themed tunes. Take turns questioning and answering. You'll be the brainiest group around for miles!

- Get mathematical proof of your expertise. For each correct answer, give yourself two points. Still not satisfied? Those tricky bonus questions earn you five more points. If you add them up without a calculator, well, you won't get any more bonus points, but you might catch NASA's attention. You expert, you.

- Make up your own *Outsmart* questions and answers. Quiz your friends and family. Enjoy the warm fuzzies that we feel right now!

Like what you've learned? Find out more about your new favorite facts by looking them up at the library. Tell 'em *Outsmart* sent you.